SEVENOAKS
1940

Sevenoaks, like many towns in England, has endured difficult years with illness, hardship and plague but, in the history of this wonderful community, one year stands out as the most traumatic ever known – 1940.

With the proximity of Fort Halstead, the fighter station of RAF Biggin Hill and the fact that the town lay on the bombers' route to London, Sevenoaks residents faced danger and death almost every day between May and December.

The population of the urban district in 1939 was 12,750 and, during the last year of peace, 178 children were born – a considerable increase on previous years. These innocent little ones came into a world of imminent conflict and those who survived would not experience peace for another five years.

Beginning with the month of July 1939 and ending on December 31st, 1940 here is the story of the drama as it unfolded in Sevenoaks and district.

Bob Ogley trading as Froglets, Brasted Chart, Westerham, Kent TN16 ILY.

Email: bob@bobogley.plus.com   ISBN 1 872337 33 3

December 2024: All rights reserved. No part of this publication may be reproduced, stored in a retrieval system or transmitted in any form or by other means, electronic, mechanical, photocopying, recording or otherwise without permission of the publisher. A catalogue record of this book is available is available from the British Library.

This book was originated by Bob Ogley (Froglets Publications) and printed and bound by Gomer Press, Llandysul, Llandysul Enterprise Park, SA44 4JL.

Front cover: The junction of London Road and High Street, Sevenoaks.

Back cover: Sevenoaks High Street showing the Holmesdale Tavern and Timothy Whites and Taylors.

One memory shared by the people who lived in Sevenoaks during the Battle of Britain in 1940 was the sight of vapour trails, or contrails, in the sky. This picture was taken of the aerial activity above Ide Hill with the spire of St Mary's Church clearly visible.

A high altitude aerial dogfight was taking place. It looks like a pastoral scene but the contrails were being created by fighter planes flown by pilots who were trying to kill each other. Hence they would be climbing and diving, twisting and turning in an attempt to out-manoeuvre each other.

The trails would start and stop as they climbed in and out of contrail altitude. Those who lived on the higher ground in the Sevenoaks villages would have known that these were skirmishes on the way to London, where the real action was taking place.

This aerial view of Sevenoaks was taken in 1956 – 16 years after the bombs fell in the town centre. It clearly shows how the High Street and London Road diverge, with the Shambles in the central section long before it was redesigned. In this picture work is underway on the improvement of Buckhurst Lane which was so badly bombed in 1940. Lime Tree Walk is top left of this photograph but the site of Club Hall and the Vine Gardens are not visible. Close to the bottom of the picture are the condemned cottages of Redman's Alley which eventually made way for the Waitrose supermarket and car park.

July 15th 1939 --50 days before war is declared.

Few people will have heard of Bushes Lane, Sevenoaks, a road of terraced cottages built in the mid-19th century and then part of a small community known as Hartslands. Today Bushes Lane is better known as Prospect Road in an area of St John's that once contained arable fields separated from the town by open countryside. The town gas works lay on the edge of Hartslands and, nearby, there were two small schools, St John's and Bayham Road. Other roads in Hartslands were Cobden Road, Cedar Terrace, Bethel Road and Quaker's Hall Lane.

The houses of two-up and two-down were occupied mostly by working class people with an average of five per home which meant that some families took in lodgers to help pay the bills. A midwife lived in one cottage in Bushes Lane and the money she earned from her skills certainly helped to improve the family income.

I was one of the children she brought into this world on July 15th 1939 (St. Swithin's Day), just 50 days before the outbreak of the Second World War. For my mother Florence May Ogley (née Reardon) it was a time of confusion, uncertainty and fear. Air raid shelters were being constructed, decontamination centres opened and refuge rooms gas-proofed, because most people were convinced that poisonous gasses, used in the trenches in 1917, would be a feature of this modern conflict. My father, John Roberts Ogley, a chemist, was part of the local team of gas-identification officers.

Of course, I was too young to understand anything about this or the growing tension that caused my mother to smoke cigarettes for the first time. Her preferred choice was du Maurier so-called after the famous British actor, Gerald. In that month of my birth, with Sevenoaks teetering on the brink of war, blackouts were being fitted in every home, motorists ordered to drive with side-lights only and sign posts were removed. We were told that stiff penalties faced those who did not comply with the regulations. The first victim of the blackout occurred the day before I was born when a young motorcyclist collided with a car at the bottom of Polhill. The car driver told the inquest he was hugging the kerb in the blackout and did not see the motorbike.

The Sevenoaks Chronicle and the Sevenoaks News were competing strongly for the best local news stories and that mid-July week did not disappoint. A man from London, who had taken part in smash-and-grab raids on a jewellers' shop belonging to John Holgate in Sevenoaks High Street and a sub post office in London Road, was committed for trial by Sevenoaks Magistrates. The furniture depositary of Messrs Quinnell and Son in St Johns had been badly damaged by fire, and lightning had hit a house in Serpentine Road.

Twelve paragraphs were given to the story of a young motorcyclist from Sevenoaks who had driven down Chart Lane, Brasted at more than 50 miles an hour and a whole column devoted to the Riverhead gardeners who had excelled in the Riverhead Sweet Pea and Rose Show. Tucked away on page four was a story of Sevenoaks Welfare Committee's lack of preparation in Sevenoaks in the event of war.

The committee had discussed the possibility of children from London being sent to Sevenoaks and the lack of air-raid shelters. Where would they go in the event of a raid? Were there enough trenches with concrete lining for schools in the district? The headmistress of

Lorries of sand from the sand pits at Greatness were dumped outside Sevenoaks Hospital and the children joined in the task of filling them. This back-breaking work required a day off school but it was also great fun.

Cobden Road School, who had been invited to speak to the committee, said that all schools should be closed in the event of a national emergency and families should not be broken up. On this day of my birth a great discussion was taking place at the council offices in Argyle Road over the "compulsory powers" of the town's billeting officer in the event of children being evacuated to Sevenoaks. On arrival at Tubs Hill station it was agreed that 14 stewards should be on duty with the Women's Voluntary Service and at least 60 volunteers, on hand to provide refreshments. Only those residents who were ill or extremely old would be exempt from providing accommodation for the children. The billeting officers' powers were part of the 'Defence of the Realm Act'.

As Sevenoaks teetered on the brink of war, German nationals living in the area were told they would be handed over to the military courts and interned if war broke out. By Saturday September 2nd the scene in almost every road in Sevenoaks was one of hectic activity. There was a long queue at Marley Tiles in Riverhead where people were buying portable air raid shelters for £18, families were strengthening their black-out arrangements and many men were signing up to Major Cazalet's new anti-aircraft battery, the 16th Light.

The last issue of the Sevenoaks News, before war was officially declared, attested to the normality of life amidst the growing chaos. The annual Three Villages Carnival (Chipstead, Riverhead and Dunton Green) had gone ahead with the proceeds in aid of the Sevenoaks and Holmesdale Hospital. A record number of local girls had been nominated to compete for the title of Carnival Queen and the winner was Miss Betty Clark of Garden Cottage, West Heath. Her attendants were Rose Ball, Jessie Box, Faith Simmons and Florence Sears.

Donald Hooper, editor of the News wrote: "The three villages handed that man, A.H. the complete cold shoulder. There were more people lining the route than in previous years although the line of procession was shorter, for lorries had been requisitioned. It was crisis carnival all right but just as happy an event as usual."

The London children seem jolly enough on the weekend that war broke out, even though they were placed in the cattle pens at Sevenoaks Market, seen as a humiliation by the many of the mothers who had travelled with them.

The main story on page one was not the appeal to women to make the evacuation of children a great success, or propaganda letters addressed to prominent Sevenoaks businessmen, arriving from Germany, or an appeal from Major Cazalet for men over 50 to join his new battery, but the fact that a man from Seal Road, Sevenoaks had been sentenced to five months hard labour for obtaining, by false pretences, the sum of five shillings!

When Prime Minister Neville Chamberlain announced we were at war with Germany, on September 3rd, I was in a cot in the front room of our flat in Sevenoaks High Street. The nerves of everyone were soon put to the most strenuous test when air raid sirens warned that raiders were on their way across Kent. As people made their way calmly to the shelters the

Sevenoaks police station and magistrates court was in the High Street and it was deemed necessary to protect the building with sandbags, a process that took many hours to complete with volunteers helping the authorities to fill the bags and then putting them carefully into place. It was a good move because the station was close to the Club Hall theatre, later to be completely destroyed in a bombing raid.

Three small children, near Valence are watching George Rudd's steam-traction engine-driven threshing machine at work in September 1939. The boxes over their shoulders contained their gas masks. In the background is the church of St. Mary's, Westerham and the churchyard. The days of peace were rapidly drawing to a close.

20-minute war claimed its first victim. Robert Frederick Leigh, a butcher, aged 25 got into a wobble on his motorbike and fell off. He abandoned his machine near the drive to Everlands, Bayleys Hill, and walked home feeling very dazed. Dr Roffey of Bessels Green was called and diagnosed a fracture of the skull. Robert Leigh was transferred to the Sevenoaks and Holmesdale Hospital where he died on Monday morning.

Churches in Sevenoaks were packed on the Sunday morning of the Prime Minister's announcement but, as the ministers from the pulpits announced that we were at war with Germany, the sirens sounded indicating that an air raid was imminent. It was, of course, a false alarm but that was unknown to the majority of people. Wardens and ARP workers in the churches left at once and mothers with children hurried home.

The Rev F.W. Argyle brought his service to a close but then conducted Holy Communion after the "all clear" sounded. The Rev Thomas Jarrett of Sevenoaks Congregational Church took his congregation to Walthamstow Hall School so they could hear the Prime Minister's statement. The 'air raid' warning prompted them to rush into the corridors anticipating the sound of bombs.

The Rev White of Vine Baptist Church was reading the Prime Minister's statement when the warning sounded. Those without children remained in the church and sat quietly, perhaps a little nervously, waiting for the service to continue. There was no pause at all in the churches of St Thomas's, where Father Phillips was conducting, or St John's Church where the Rev Hawkes just carried on. The sirens, however, sent a few people scampering home from the Drive Methodist Church. There was no real panic anywhere. The people of Sevenoaks, as the editor of the News had predicted, were giving Adolf the "cold shoulder".

By the evening of Sunday September 2nd Sevenoaks had received most of its quota of London evacuees. The operation was smooth for the organisers but painful and humiliating for the children who were placed in the sheep pens in Sevenoaks Market where they waited until being transferred to local homes. Some waited longer than others. They all wore warm coats, labelled with name and address and school number. It had been a hot weekend.

The final batch of children arrived on Tuesday taking the total to almost 7,000. The children from London then settled down to a strange life in a country town unaware that it would be many months before the real action began.

The largest group of all came from Shooter's Hill School. The boys aged between 11 and 17 were billeted in homes in upper Sevenoaks, and Kippington Grange was requisitioned by the urban council as a temporary school. They would not have known that their stay in Sevenoaks was to last five years and a few would join the local Home Guard. The activity in Sevenoaks during this first week under war clouds was exceptional in the history of the town. Firemen based at the central station in Eardley Road remained on duty night and day with two engines and a Beresford Stork trailer pump. Fire patrols were on readiness at the Royal Oak Hotel, Pinewood Garage and the ARP store in Robyns Way. In addition to members of the regular brigade, 54 fully-trained auxiliary fire men were on standby.

The 14 air raid warden posts in Sevenoaks were also manned all night and, should air raids become frequent, plans were made for an all-day presence. Among the warden's posts were those at Walthamstow Hall School, Bradbourne Stables, Sevenoaks Waterworks, the White House in the High Street, the Railway Tavern and Tonbridge Road Nurseries.

Members of VAD (Kent 76) stood by at St John's Ambulance hut and St Nicholas parish hall in Lime Tree Walk. The public utility services -- gas, water and electricity -- in Sevenoaks were fully protected with sandbags and camouflage at the pumping stations and reservoirs in Oak Lane, Cramptons Road and Kemsing. The train services from Tubs Hill and Bat and Ball were running to schedule, many packed with troops and evacuees. All First Aid posts were fully manned and bus services from Sevenoaks were back to normal, except for the Green line coaches which had been commandeered as ambulances.

Sevenoaks urban council published a list of shelters for members of the public who could be caught in an air raid while shopping, or away from their own home. They included those at Leslie Warren opticians, Messrs S. Young and Son furniture store, Russell and Bromley (all in the High Street) the Old Brewery in Brewery Lane, Stanley's Garage, Vine and St John's Methodist Church. In this first wartime issue of the Sevenoaks News the only advertisements came from S. Young and Son who were promoting their back-to-school wear for boys and girls (all-wool jackets and trousers 26/-, 'Nigger' and Navy cloth coats 32/6d), and the photographer George P King who was offering reduced portrait prices for members of the armed services. Sevenoaks Hire took a half page ad promoting cars at 3d a mile and declaring that we "the Vauxhall Fusiliers don't fear Hitler."

It is difficult to imagine how anyone could think of buying a new home in the week that war broke out but Ibbett Mosely and Card advertised a three-bedroom cottage in Sevenoaks Weald for £675 and a substantial house at Wildernesse for £1,000. The only other advertisement came from the Majestic and Plaza cinemas who declared they were closed until further notice but "our cafes will remain open".

The Sevenoaks News in particular was reporting everything the public wanted to know. How posts would be manned with everyone at the ready and fully equipped, how telephonists were at their switchboards waiting for the signal, how builders were fully trained to deal with any emergencies and how the spirit of service was prompting the hand of hospitality and friendship. "This issue", it correctly predicted "will become an historic one."

Time has told us of the value of this understatement. Eight pages in the issue of September 7th 1939 were devoted to the town's preparation for the conflict that lay ahead. There were just five pictures – the arrival at Tubs Hill station of ten-week old twins in the arms of nurses, evacuated from Denmark Hill, men, women and boys tackling the heavy task of sandbagging

The Plaza cinema opened in Sevenoaks in 1937 on a site that had once been Smith's Brewery and then the Cinema Electric Theatre. A uniformed commissioner stood outside the cinema to greet patrons and inside was a plush restaurant. Some years after the war it became the Granada.

the hospital, children waiting in the cattle pens and photographs of two couples, who had made the decision to get married before hostilities began.

The issues that followed were also historic. How respirators were being provided for babies, how the elementary school population in Sevenoaks had doubled, how residents were being urged to turn their gardens into allotments and the sad stories of young people who had died in road accidents because of the black-out.

As it became clear that German bombers would not be appearing for a while the cinemas re-opened and the Plaza advertised a blockbuster – "the story of three lusty sons of the sword, reckless in love, ruthless in war and dauntless in peril". The people of Sevenoaks flocked to see Douglas Fairbanks Jnr, Cary Grant and Victor McLaglen in Gunga Din, and the war was briefly forgotten.

As the days went by and there was no sign of real hostility, life became a little more normal although there was a little bit of panic buying when petrol rationing was introduced and motorists queued for their quota at Caffyns garage. There was also a warning for children not to build and light bonfires on Guy Fawkes' night – their parents threatened with a £100 fine.

It is difficult to conjure up a mental picture of those early weeks of the war years. German U boats and submarines were deployed in the seas around Britain. Two fully trained Hurricane squadrons (79 and 32) were based at RAF Biggin Hill. Local cricket clubs had packed up for

A few Sevenoaks notables outside the Majestic cinema. The bearded gentleman (centre right) was Sir John Laurie later to become Lord Mayor of London. Also in the photograph is Rev Argyle vicar of St Nicholas, Sevenoaks.

the winter but football and rugby was being played on a Saturday. Winston Churchill had rejoined the Cabinet as First Lord of the Admiralty. Life was carrying on as normal – almost.

The Sevenoaks branch of the Anglican Pacifist Fellowship and the Sevenoaks Fellowship of Peace Groups held a joint meeting and declared: "We want Hitler's head on a charger and when we get it we will call this war off. Among the audience at the Sevenoaks Girls Club were some of the 200 refugees, many of whom could not speak English. As Christmas approached more couples were walking down the aisle, some with just a best man, one bridesmaid and parents present. No friends, no reception, just a little music – the men knowing they would soon be called up. Among them was a Sevenoaks Chronicle reporter Victor Froud who was marrying Doris Evelyn Larkham. The couple walked out of St Nicholas Church under an archway of rolled newspapers held by all the journalists of Sevenoaks.

By late November more than 50,000 ration books had been issued to every householder in Sevenoaks (urban and rural), with a note informing them they had just a few weeks to register with their regular retailer for sugar, butter, bacon and ham. The Plaza cinema had formed a Teddy Bear Club for children and Arthur Turner of Turner's Nurseries was advising the gardeners of Sevenoaks how to look after their allotments in winter. Sevenoaks British Legion had enrolled more than 300 new members and raised a record sum from the sale of poppies on Remembrance Sunday.

"Happy Christmas to all our readers", said the Sevenoaks Chronicle and News. "Here is some good news. The Plaza and Majestic cinemas will be opening on Christmas Day, Messrs Patullo and Vinson have reported a stock of exceptional high quality at the Sevenoaks Fat Stock show and the local magistrates have granted an extension of hours (until 11pm) for pubs in the town. Inoculations against diphtheria are available at Sevenoaks Clinic and there

The bells of St Nicholas which were ordered to remain silent in 1939 had been cast at the Whitechapel Bell Foundry in 1769 and 1771. They were rung later on in the war but time gradually took its toll so in 1966 the ring of eight bells was recast at Whitechapel. Picture by Alex Watson shows them on the day they were delivered.

will be a free cinema show for all evacuees in the King's Hall, Bligh's Meadow." One sour note rang out from the tower of St Nicholas where bell-ringing practice had been suspended for the duration of war. "This is an English custom", said the chairman of the urban council Fred Goodwin. "The odds against an air-raid warning being sounded during ringing practice is 168-1 but we cannot take chances". "Who runs this town?" asked Fred Jarvis. "Police or the council? Because, if there is a war we will not all be dead and survivors are entitled to some amusement."

"It is on my shoulders to give the town a warning of a raid", said Mr Anderson. "St Nicholas is on a hill and with the variation of wind the bells could drown out the approach of enemy bombers. They WILL remain silent."

As Sevenoaks went to the church services on Christmas morning 1939 one hymn in particular had a little more meaning than most. Silent night.

1940 – The bombing of Sevenoaks

Just a spoonful of sugar, a smear of butter and a slice of bacon. That was the message to Sevenoaks housewives as the year of 1940 dawned. Don't attempt to obtain food from Eire because you will be jailed for six months, they were told. All grocery shops will be given weighing machines.

Rationing had officially begun but there was still no hint that an invasion was imminent. How could it be? Sevenoaks, like much of the country, was now in the grip of a severe winter. Snow whipped up by piercing winds from the east was heaped into huge drifts, villages on the North Downs were marooned and the supplies of food and fuel were dangerously low. The snow ploughs had been busy and huge piles lay either side of the main roads but this was a quieter January than usual.

Snow was also hampering the work of construction gangs attempting to lay a new runway at Biggin Hill and excavate deep shelters. Flying conditions were appalling but the RAF managed to keep airborne for some 100 hours a week.

The Sevenoaks cinemas remained open throughout the bitter winter providing a variety of choices for the increasing number of patrons. One of them created a huge controversy – *Hitler Beast of Berlin*. The film had been banned in America as too inflammatory and reissued in other parts of England as *Goose Step*. But at the Plaza, Sevenoaks it was being shown with its original title attacking the fundamental evils of Nazism and showing archival footage of Adolf Hitler. The cinema goers of Sevenoaks loved it, many people "goose-stepping" their way back home from the High Street.

The Sevenoaks Chronicle and the Sevenoaks News were competing strongly in providing all the relevant information for their readers. Paper, however was rationed and everyone was urged to order their copy in advance rather than buy it from the shelves.

Winston Churchill, at home in Chartwell on a summer evening in May 1940, lit one of his favourite Cuban cigars, called for his secretary Mary Shearburn and told her to take shorthand notes on a speech he was composing.

During the dictation Miss Shearburn was apparently a little perturbed by a bat which had flown into the room. Churchill told her: "Do not be concerned Miss Shearburn. I shall protect you."

A few days later in the House of Commons Churchill delivered the speech and received a standing ovation. It included perhaps his most famous lines.

"....Even though large tracts of Europe and many old and famous States have fallen or may fall into the grip of the Gestapo and all the odious apparatus of Nazi rule, we shall not flag or fail. We shall go on to the end, we shall fight in France, we shall fight on the seas and oceans, we shall fight with growing confidence and growing strength in the air, we shall defend our Island, whatever the cost may be, we shall fight on the beaches, we shall fight on the landing grounds, we shall fight in the fields and in the streets, we shall fight in the hills; we shall never surrender...."

It was a speech, according to one MP, "worth 1,000 guns."

Elizabeth Layton joined the Chartwell staff as a secretary a few months later. In her memoirs she recalled how Churchill would dictate late into the night, sometimes until 4.30 am, "ruminating around his room in his red, green and gold dressing gown."

Churchill employed many secretaries during his years at Chartwell and as Prime Minister. During the making of a cinema biopic *Darkest Hour,* many years later, Elizabeth Layton was credited as the secretary who took the dictation of this famous speech. In fact it was Mary Shearburn who had been at Chartwell before war broke out.

It was there she met Walter Thompson, a local police detective who had been invited to protect Churchill at night for the salary of £5 a week

"I was told to collect Churchill's Colt revolver from Mary", he later wrote. "But she refused to hand it over. I produced identification and she eventually handed it over. It had been fitted with a new trigger and cross-pin as well as having the barrel re-jointed."

He wrote: "I went on patrol in the house and gardens of Chartwell. "It was quiet in the Kentish countryside but I was ready to pounce upon a would-be Nazi murderer."

Mary and Walter, Churchill's bodyguard, were married after the war.

By the spring, scores of local boys serving with the British Expeditionary Force (BEF) in Belgium were writing letters back home, their cheerfulness giving little hint of the fact that the Germans were closing in. A few of them seemed delighted that Winston Churchill was forming a new administration after his appointment as Prime Minister telling his MPs that "I have nothing to offer but blood, sweat, toil and tears."

His words took on a real meaning when Vice Admiral Bertram Russell, deep in his underground bunker within the cliffs of Dover, gave the order for the emergency evacuation of troops from the beaches of Dunkirk, some 70 miles away across the Channel. The boys, writing back home, hardly mentioned Operation Dynamo but they knew they were trapped and would have to make their way to the beaches and take part in what was to become one of the most extraordinary military manoeuvres in history.

The many Sevenoaks families with fathers and sons in Belgium would not have known that Group Captain Victor Goddard of Meadowbank, Brasted Chart had been ordered to fly from France with a message from General Gort, Commander-in-chief of the BEF that Royal Navy destroyers and other vessels were insufficient to lift the troops off the beaches. Ramsay responded positively and summoned the little ships.

Not all the local boys made it back home. A few were killed in the evacuation and several captured. Many made it across the Channel and, once in Dover or Folkestone, alerted their families. Private D.W. Ritchie of Buckhurst Avenue wrote: "I am on a train somewhere in England. Handing this note out of the window at the next railway station hoping it will reach you."

Mrs Lowing of Witches Lane, Bessels Green received a card from her husband saying he was back in 'Blighty' and looking forward to meeting his three-week old son. Private John Terry of Bosville Drive simply wrote: "I am home from Flanders." He didn't know that on that very day his brother Ron had been called to the colours.

Sevenoaks urban councillor Mrs William Daws and her husband, who ran a plumbing business in Sevenoaks, heard news that their youngest son had successfully reached England. Herbert Turner of Weald Road had also reached England but his brother Roger, serving with the RAF, had died in a raid on the Kiel Canal.

The boys who reached Dover on one of the rescue ships found trains waiting at the station to take the men back to their units. Dover had 327 trains and moved 180,982 men; Ramsgate carried 783 men on 82 trains; 64 were supplied at Folkestone; 75 at Margate and 17 at Sheerness. Headcorn and Paddock Wood stations were used as eight minute food stops.

One serving soldier who managed to get back home to Dunton Green was Trooper R.F. Robbins of the Tank Corps. As he was enjoying breakfast with his wife a telegram boy knocked on the door with a message "Regret Trooper Robbins is missing."

Parted from his unit this Sevenoaks footballer had made his own way to Bergues 10 miles from Dunkirk. He found an abandoned lorry and with three others made his way to the beaches. Although bombs fell on the vehicle and two were injured Trooper Robbins was able to reach Dunkirk. Another late arrival was Ian Audsley, a young furniture maker, destined to set up a successful business in Sevenoaks. He was possibly the last man to be rescued.

With the men away at war the women of Sevenoaks took over many of their jobs such as postmen, milkmen, butchers and, of course, land army girls.

Many of the boys who reached their homes in Sevenoaks found Union Jacks and Welcome Home banners pinned to the front gate or wall of their homes. One was Guardsman James Berry, 21, who had suffered a shrapnel wound when the beaches were bombed but he limped on to a ship and became just one of the 338,226 British and Allied troops to make it home. By June Local Defence Volunteer units had been formed all over the country and particularly in Kent, where it was anticipated the enemy would land. Scores of local men between the ages of 17 and 65 had made the journey to Wildernesse Country Club, or Knole Park Golf Club to sign on. The men had no uniforms, received no pay, or expenses and were told they would have to share rifles and ammunition.

They were told they were part of a Citizens' Army which contained not only 17-year-old boys but bank managers, shop owners and former officers, who had fought in the Great War. The men drilled night after night in the Drill Hall, Argyle Road and were told they were to observe and report on all enemy movements and to defend all roads and positions vital to the preservation of Sevenoaks and district. In time, of course, they would be known as the Home Guard.

In early July, Edith Oliver, daughter of Fred Oliver of the Railway Tavern, Bat and Ball was walking across the Vine cricket ground when she saw a large piece of paper floating to the ground. She picked it up and there, to her surprise, was a message from Adolf Hitler appealing for reason from the people of Britain to avert "destruction of a great world empire. Rejection would mean an attack with all of the forces at the command of the Axis powers."

This, of course, was a propaganda leaflet dropped from a German plane with the speech the Fuehrer had made to the German Reichstag. They were found scattered in towns all over England. Edith, a 40-year-old spinster, returned home, quietly put the pathetic but historic message in a folder and the next day travelled to London to get on with her job with the Young Women's Christian Association. When she died in 1990, aged 90, the message from Hitler was discovered among her possessions.

With the proximity of RAF Biggin Hill and dummy airfields at Lullingstone and Fort Halstead, the war had now reached Sevenoaks and, as the Battle of Britain began on July 1st, the people of Sevenoaks had a ringside seat. Day after day Spitfires and Hurricanes would suddenly appear from the direction of the North Downs on their way to intercept the German bombers which were flying in V formation and usually escorted from the rear and above by Messerschmitt 109s and 110s.

Children on holiday from Sevenoaks and district were able to see much of the action although many were encouraged to take cover in the shelters. It was the start of the most dramatic and tragic months that the town and villages had ever known.

German aircraft were falling out of the sky at regular intervals, shot down by our fighters from Biggin Hill and Kenley. Many crashed in the Kent villages including those in the Sevenoaks area. The skies above the village of Ide Hill, especially, became a major battlefield and the village schoolchildren, without an air raid shelter, were constantly diving under their desks to take cover when the sirens sounded. One of the great pictures, later published in national newspapers throughout the world, shows the church spire of Ide Hill silhouetted against the Battle of Britain vapour trails (see page 2).

August 16, 1940

In August a Heinkel was forced down in a field near Sundridge Hospital – prompting men and women from the village of Ide Hill to race to the scene. They found an uninjured German pilot showing his displeasure at the fate which had befallen him. Excited onlookers now wondered how long it would be before another German aircraft would crash in the village. They didn't have to wait long. Two days later, on August 18th, a Junkers 88A of a Luftwaffe bomber group, *Kampfgeschwader 76 (KG 76)*.was shot down and burst into flames near St Mary's Church.

Six Battle of Britain pilots each claimed it was their "kill" -- Flight Lieutenant J.G. Sanders of 615 Squadron, Pilot Officers A.F. Laws, J.J. O'Meara and E.G. Gilbert of 64 Squadron, Flight Lieutenant P.M. Brothers and Pilot Officer B. Wlasnowolski of 32 Squadron. So difficult was it to reach a correct conclusion it was decided on the following -- Gilbert, Laws and O'Meara each awarded a '½ kill' and Sanders, Brothers and Wlasnowolski each a kill. Thus the Ide Hill Junkers was counted 4½ times in the overall British victory total for that day.

To this day no-one has ever discovered the name of the successful pilot, leading Battle of Britain experts to conclude that the pilots' shooting ability was more accurate than their aircraft identification.

What is not disputed is the fact that the German crew -- Oberfw A. Eichhorn, Stabsfw H. Vetter, Fw K. Geier and Gefr K. Skuthan were all killed

Flight Lieutenant Peter Brothers (later to rise through the ranks) was living with his wife-to-be Annette and her mother, Eve Wilson in a house opposite Pitts Cottage, Westerham

By August 1940 Sevenoaks had its own efficient looking LDV (Local Defence Volunteers). They were badly equipped but well briefed on the assumption they would soon be fighting German parachutists and providing military protection at all points of importance. Here are a few of the men outside the Drill Hall in Argyle Road, Sevenoaks.

It was on that memorable Sunday that the sirens of Sevenoaks were put to their first big test. Many took cover as nine Dornier bombers, on their way to Biggin Hill, were met by the Hurricanes of 32 Squadron. Hundreds of high explosives fell and huge craters pockmarked the airfield and the woods of the North Downs. The storm had broken.

The men, women and children of Sevenoaks, now gripped by fear waited for the next assault. They didn't have to wait long. During the next evening five separate formations converged over the town and the sirens wailed, sending many Sevenoaks people into the shelters they were to know so well. In the half light of their underground refuge they heard the noise above as stick after stick of incendiaries rained down.

Day after day, night after night it continued and everyone became accustomed to the routine of scrambles, sightings, interceptions and vapour trails. Then there were barrage balloons over the North Downs, glowing in the southern sun, smooth and silver against the constant blue skies of 1940. For many they were at their most beautiful by moonlight, many sometimes whistling as the cables which attached them to the ground stirred in the night breeze.

Not to be deterred by the threat from the skies cricket in Sevenoaks and the villages was now being played again. On August 31st, Sevenoaks Vine entertained Richmond and a local solicitor Clive Russell Vick, later to become a partner at Knocker and Foskett, scored a magnificent century. Five times the game was interrupted by air raids sending the players and spectators into the basement of the Sennocke Engineering Company. Five times the game continued as if nothing had happened.

The distinctive white cross on the hill was blacked out when Shoreham played Farningham in August 1940 and it remained covered up for the duration of the war years.

August 24, 1940

Cricket was played on the Vine during the Battle of Britain and in most of the villages, including Shoreham, later to be known worldwide as "bomb alley".

On August 24th, 1940 when the Battle of Britain was approaching its deadliest stage, Shoreham entertained Farningham and, because of the proximity of the two villages, their most deadly rivals. The match began with the distinctive white cross on the hill blacked out so it could not be seen by any raider. But the players, adhering to the accepted cricketing attire, wore white.

Farningham -- one short and without regular wicket-keeper Harry Acton -- batted first. They had just settled in to their innings when one umpire, looking at the hilltop horizon rather than down the wicket, sensed that "Jerry was about", although so intent was the concentration on the game that no-one could recall hearing any warning air-raid siren.

After an over in which a series of increasingly loud thumps, bumps and bangs were heard, play was suspended while everyone watched a terrific aerial battle going on some way to the north. The players eventually drifted back towards the pavilion, where there was considerable discussion on the wisdom of continuing while dog-fights went on overhead, accompanied by anti-aircraft and machine-gun fire, shell-bursts and falling shrapnel.

However, the match eventually resumed and Farningham were obliged to declare their innings closed at 80 for six because they were now four short. The men hadn't run away because of the action overhead but had reported for duty in the Home Guard. Of the

Shoreham team, only Frank Chatfield had to excuse himself on the grounds he was a special constable.

Shoreham passed the total with just three wickets down and the teams, as usual later retired for a post-match drink in The George, with the Farningham players arguing that Hitler's tactics that day had robbed them of a fair chance of completing victory over Shoreham.

Later that night bombs fell on London for the first time and in retaliation, Churchill ordered Berlin to be bombed the following night. Within a fortnight the Blitz of London had begun, the western sky over the Downs glowing red as bombs and incendiaries rained down on both Darenth Valley villages.

By the end of August 1940, the Luftwaffe had virtually lost the Battle of Britain and the German air fleets (Luftflotten) were ordered to attack London, to draw RAF Fighter Command into a battle of annihilation. Adolf Hitler and Reichsmarschall Hermann Göering, commander-in-chief of the Luftwaffe, ordered the new policy on September 6th, and it was on the following day that the bombers flew over Sevenoaks on their way to London.

Before they ceased the attacks on airfields, however, the Luftwaffe had made a new attempt to destroy RAF Biggin Hill and on the evening of August 3rd, a small formation of Junkers caused the greatest damage and loss of life the station would ever experience. One bomb hit the airmen's shelter and killed 39 people. Others destroyed the cookhouses, workshops, the NAAFI, the sergeants' mess, 90 per cent of the station's transport and two Spitfires.

The relentless pounding of Biggin Hill continued until September 2nd – the sixth raid in 48 hours. By then there was little left to destroy save the unquenchable spirit of the personnel and the fact that the airfield itself was "still operational."

For 56 of the following 64 days and nights London was systematically bombed and the people of Sevenoaks and district were witnesses to the wave of Junkers, Heinkels and Dorniers which passed over the town, generally at night. The most destructive attacks were two daylight raids one on September 15th and another on December 29th, which resulted in a firestorm, later known as the Second Great Fire of London.

September 6, 1940

Less than a week after the Biggin Hill tragedy Sevenoaks had a sighting of a real dog fight in which a German Dornier and a Spitfire Mk1 were locked in deadly combat over the North Downs. To the shock of those watching the two planes collided. The bomber dived into the River Darent near the offices of the Sevenoaks Electricity Company at Sundridge. One of the German crew baled out and was later arrested in Westerham. His three colleagues were killed.

The Spitfire pilot Pat Hughes (left), an Australian of 244 Squadron, crashed at Dark's Farm, Dry Hill Lane, Bessels Green and was killed. On that day the greatest attacking force yet seen flew across Kent on its way to London – a staggering total of 338 bombers and 617 fighters across a 20-mile front. The men on the observer posts could hardly believe their eyes.

September 28, 1940

On Saturday September 28th, 1940 a number of guests attended Crowborough Church to see a young British pilot, 27-year-old Lionel Schwind and his wife, Georgina reaffirm their vows. Among the guests was Lionel's father who had not been able to attend their wedding in Edinburgh in December 1939.

As the congregation gathered one person was missing – the groom. Lionel, a flight lieutenant with 213 Squadron at Tangmere had been killed the previous day and the news did not reach his family in time to alert the congregation. It is possible his Squadron officers did not know of his special day, or the fact that Georgina was pregnant (their daughter Penelope was born in June 1941).

News of the tragedy was relayed to all the guests. Lionel Schwind's Squadron, patrolling the Sussex coast, had intercepted an attacking force of Messerschmitt 110s over Gatwick. In the ensuing dogfight his Hurricane was hit in the tail and began to burn. Unable to bale out he gradually lost height and crashed in Chance Wood on the Wildernesse Golf Course. This was the second tragedy in the family.

Lionel's brother, Sgt Gordon Schwind, an Air Observer with 59 Squadron had been killed when his Blenheim was shot down in May 1940, near Dussen in the Netherlands. He was buried in a cemetery in Hainault, Belgium.

Lionel's funeral was held at All Saints Church, Crowborough on October 4th, 1941 with full military honours. It was 40 years later, in 1980 that a memorial to Lionel was erected on Wildernesse Golf Course.

September 21, 1940

Walthamstow Hall School, in Holly Bush Lane, Sevenoaks, had played a big role in the weeks leading up to the Battle of Britain, as a clearing home for evacuees and then an Air Raid Wardens' post in which members of the teaching staff shared a fire-watching rota each night. During the summer raids of 1940 lessons and exams continued in the shelters with children sitting on their bunk beds.

It was uncomfortable but wise. On the night of September 21st, 1940 the school's new laboratory, craft rooms and old gymnasium were destroyed by bombs and damage caused to the whole school. No-one was hurt but it was a terrifying night clearly remembered by those who were pupils at the time.

One of them, Shirley Legge (née Salmon), a 10-year-old boarder at Wally Hall (as the school was always known) said: "Because of the air raids the girls slept downstairs for safety. On that night I was with four girls in reception and we slept on the floor with a bundle of emergencies which we used as pillows.

"Bread-baskets fell in pairs and when the first dropped nearby I remember standing up while the others slept. When the second fell on the Science Block the wire netted window frame flew past me and landed on the girl furthest away. I snatched my bundle and went into the hall to find Nurse standing with stained glass from the dome in the ceiling sprinkling down on her. I think I fainted; all I remember is suddenly being in an air raid shelter with all the domestic staff — and no girls.

"Much later I was told to walk to the front of the school where taxis were waiting to take everyone to a community centre in Sevenoaks. As I climbed into the last taxi I heard my name being called and my father appeared at the window of the taxi. To this day I can remember the joy. Unbeknown to me my parents had come down from London to give me a surprise the next day and were staying with friends in Dartford Road.

"Looking back across the playing fields it appeared as if the whole school was on fire. The girls were then distributed around Sevenoaks. I briefly went to stay with a Dr Taylor but my mother had insisted that we should be together in Dartford Road and I was picked up again by taxi. On the way another bomb dropped which lifted the taxi from the road onto the grass verge. We continued with our journey and later discovered that the bomb had damaged Dr Taylor's house but no-one was hurt.

"Next day I remember standing in the garden at Dartford Road watching a 'dog fight' in the clear blue skies. To the horror of everyone we saw an RAF pilot who had been shot down being fired on by a German fighter as he descended in his parachute".

Shirley went to stay with her Godmother in Staffordshire until Walthamstow Hall found somewhere to evacuate the girls. The boarders were eventually taken to Pontisford House on

The gymnasium at Walthamstow Hall School destroyed by German bombs in September 1940. 35 girls escaped uninjured.

the west side of Shewsbury. Another Wally Hall old girl, Dorothy Slater described the night of September 24th, 1940 in a letter to her friend Katherine Mitchell. Part of it read: "School has been bombed well and thoroughly but we're all safe. It's a mercy that Kent had postponed the opening of school till the 30th, so there were only about 35 of us girls — and about 70 altogether including staff and maids.

"It happened just before 9pm Saturday night. There was a magnetic mine, 8ft by 2ft on the top of the field killing the new pullets and doing a terrific amount of damage. We have the parachute of it as a souvenir of wonderful silk and cords in a pile which takes four men to lift. Also a high explosive fell on the gym wrecking it horribly and then, worst of all, a stick of incendiary bombs fell on the craft room, science room block all of which burned to the ground and there are now only the charred remains of the foundations."

Dorothy went on to describe the terrific explosion and the commotion which followed and how the 13 girls sleeping in the lecture room were confronted with hysterical maids, some bleeding, whose flat had been badly damaged. She said "that Sister was rendering first aid frantically and the ARP men were marvellous and on the spot at once. Ram (Miss Ramsay, the headmistress) was wonderful --- at her best in such an emergency."

Although Sevenoaks had no direct or military significance the bombing continued and so did the death toll. By the end of September 1940 Sevenoaks had endured a dozen raids, with many injured and taken to the Holmesdale and Sevenoaks Cottage Hospital, where nurses worked overtime without any extra remuneration.

September 27, 1940

When a huge force of Junkers 88s missed the rendezvous with their fighter escorts on September 27th, 1940 the German pilots foolishly decided to press on towards London unprotected. Hurricanes and Spitfires were scrambled to meet them and, like a pack of hounds, cornered a dozen bombers and picked them off, one by one.

The first broke up over Cudham and came down near Dorking. Five plunged into the Channel and others crashed at East Grinstead, Horsmonden, Penshurst and Sevenoaks. Another, badly maimed, flew on towards the Thames Estuary.

On this Friday afternoon there were plenty of people in Sevenoaks High Street and London Road watching the dog fight above. At 3.30 pm one of the German bombers, singled out by fighters from Biggin Hill, suddenly nose-dived towards the town with scores of people scampering for the nearest shelter as the pilot of the blazing wreck struggled with his controls.

Wartime restrictions on reporting did not apply on this occasion, as the victim was an enemy aircraft, so the story appeared in full in the Sevenoaks Chronicle issue of Friday October 4th, 1940.

An eyewitness from Sevenoaks described how the Junkers machine suddenly became a raging inferno and left behind an ever increasing trail of smoke. From vantage points the machine was seen to be heading towards the town with pieces coming down in a shower. The Junkers just missed a house near Knole Paddock and then appeared to blow up in mid-air. A cloud of dense smoke filled the air and, in the midst of this, a tattered parachute with an obviously lifeless body hanging on to it.

Quickly it crashed to earth and, in the explosion, the tailpiece came away and landed in the road which leads from the Knole Way approach to the Paddock and the Plymouth Lodge entrance to Knole. One engine crashed into the field between Seal Hollow and the Holly Bush Lane recreation ground. The rest of the plane landed against fir trees near the end of the putting green. Red hot pieces fell on the Sevenoaks Bowling Green, burning many patches in the Cumberland turf.

Play was later possible on four of the six rinks.

The Junkers had miraculously missed all the houses and shops, skimmed over Seal Hollow Road and hit the ground on the northern side of Holly Bush Lane recreation ground near the Hole in the Wall gate to Knole Park. Oblt Seif, Uffz Gebhardt and Fw Eichinger were killed immediately. Fw Zinsmeister, who had baled out was captured, badly wounded, near Sevenoaks Weald.

The drama co-incided with end-of-school lessons for the day and, within minutes, boys from Sevenoaks Prep School, Bayham Road and Sevenoaks School and a few girls from Walthamstow Hall had arrived at the scene. Wardens had cordoned off the crash site but remnants of the crippled aircraft were everywhere and the souvenir hunters were enjoying rich pickings.

In September 1940 a Junkers 88 came down near Holly Bush Lane recreation ground and red hot pieces of metal from the wreck burned holes in the Cumberland turf of Sevenoaks Bowling Green. The Chronicle reported at the time that play was later possible on four rinks, providing a wonderful example of the defiance shown in 1940. Here are the ladies of Sevenoaks playing bowls on the same rink 25 years later.

However, the drama was not over. The Chronicle wrote: "Not only was it a grim scene, it was dangerous. Machine gun bullets shot forth in their hundreds and firemen and spectators were obliged to take what shelter the trees could afford them. Fortunately no-one was injured."

My older brother Roy Ogley was one who remembered the drama. He didn't pick up any aircraft bits but the next day a boy brought a small matchbox to school, opened it and proudly showed part of a severed finger.

Andrew McDowall, a pupil at Sevenoaks Prep in Vine Court Road in 1940, later wrote: "I will always remember when a German bomber crashed into the playing fields near Walthamstow Hall. At the end of school trophy hunters, of which there were many, rushed to the crash site and recovered all kinds of aircraft bits. One boy found a human arm which he was proudly showing when the police arrived and, thankfully, confiscated it."

On this memorable day the twelfth crippled Junkers was chased towards the Thames Estuary by pilots of 66 and 92 Squadrons. What happened next turned out to be one of the most fascinating stories of the war.

Piloted by Underoffizer Fritz Ruhlandt, the bomber crash-landed on the Graveney marshes, just a few hundred yards from the Sportsman Inn on the South Oaze sea wall. The wounded

The Junkers which crashed on Romney Marsh. Soldiers of the Irish Rifles are seen here with the local policeman and children.

captain and his crew crawled out of the aircraft and were immediately confronted by troops of the 1st London Irish Rifles who happened to be billeted in the Sportsman Inn. Imagine the surprise of the soldiers when the German airmen opened fire with two machine guns and a sub machine gun just as they were preparing to arrest the crew.

The captain in charge deployed his men in a line and they crawled along the dykes prepared for a vicious land battle. When they were within 100 yards one of the Junkers crew waved a white flag. The soldiers pounced and there was a fight but as they were taken away one by one Captain John Cantopher heard one of them say in German that "the aircraft could go up anytime now".

Captain Cantopher found the time bomb, successfully defused it and joined his men and the crew of the Junkers at the Sportsman Inn where they were all enjoying a drink. Cantopher was later awarded the Military Medal.

Many years later this skirmish between the German bomber crew and the London Irish Riflemen was officially recognised as the last military conflict to be fought on British soil. More than 120 men of the Irish Rifles Regimental Association marched the few hundred yards from the scene of the battle to The Sportsman where a plaque was unveiled.

Most history books have Bonnie Prince Charlie's defeat at Culloden in 1746 as the last pitched battle fought on British soil. In fact, it was at Graveney Marshes 194 years later. The boys of Sevenoaks Prep School and their friends knew nothing about this at the time. They were still hunting for treasure in Holly Bush Lane.

During the 1939-45 war years the Sevenoaks Bowls Club continued to function. The games went on as usual and were only briefly interrupted by the giant German bomber which crash-landed in close proximity to the green, during a Saturday night raid. Fortunately, it caused very little damage to the recreation ground. George Castle, one of the Sevenoaks bowlers, who was in the local constabulary, escorted the three members of the crew to the Police Station. On another occasion, when German incendiary bombs landed on the green, without exploding, George was just in time to prevent army personnel from digging unnecessarily large holes in the green to recover possible bombs.

The Royal Oak, Wrotham Heath which received a direct hit on the night of October 15th, 1940.

Eleven villagers and an airman were killed on this, the most tragic night of the war in the Sevenoaks district

October 15, 1940

Public houses remained open during the darkest days of the blitz and one of them was the Royal Oak at Wrotham Heath. On the night of October 15th, 1940 several locals watching, or taking place, in a darts match heard the familiar drone as more than 400 enemy aircraft passed overhead on their way to the London docks.

In the kitchen, Harriet Fread, the 80-year-old mother-in-law of Jack Swift, the licensee of the pub, was busy making sandwiches with the kitchen maids Margaret Breeds and Mary Ann Fisher.

Sometime later, at 9.37, a German raider, on the return leg of its sortie, dropped 16 sticks of high explosives over the village. The first explosive scored a direct hit on the Royal Oak pub, penetrating the kitchen and killing Harriet Fread and Margaret Breeds (Mary Ann Fisher escaped with shock). The blast tore through the premises, devastating the bar and taking the lives of Frederick Walter Heine and Frederick Whiteman, who both died trapped under rubble.

An aircraftman, John Mansell, stationed at RAF Detling, who had stopped in for a pint, was also killed and a number of other locals received injuries. Customers in the saloon bar were showered with glass and bomb fragments.

Several bombs also fell at Wrotham Heath House and Hester McInnes, who was visiting her mother, died sitting in an armchair in front of the fireplace. Her mother's companion, Olive Hodgson, was also killed. Bombs peppered the London Road (A20) damaging Rootes filling station, which was situated next to the pub.

In total, 11 locals and one airman lost their lives on this horrific night in Wrotham. In London, it had been the worst toll since the opening days of the Blitz, and as dawn broke on November 16th, 400 were dead, and over 900 wounded.

The Holmesdale Tavern, a favourite wartime pub for the soldiers.

October 17, 1940

If ever there was a day to remember (or perhaps forget) in the history of Sevenoaks then it must be Thursday October 17th, 1940. It was autumn and the long, hot summer of constant blue skies had given way to rain and cloud but the leaves were still on the trees. At Biggin Hill the destruction of the airfield was almost complete with the married quarters uninhabitable and the roads and runways cratered. The 'Ops' room had moved into an empty shop but, miraculously, the airfield remained operational.

In London the roof of St Paul's had been shattered but services were being held every day. St Thomas' hospital, badly damaged, continued with operations. The Stock Exchange was hit but never closed.

Neither did our local cinemas, the Majestic and Plaza, which were allowed to remain open throughout the darkest days of the Battle of Britain. They had been encouraged perhaps by George Bernard Shaw who, in a letter to the Times newspaper, had written: "What agent of Chancellor Hitler is it who has suggested that we should all cower in darkness and terror for the duration?"

For just a week in September 1939 Sevenoaks had been denied cinema entertainment but they quickly re-opened despite the fact that they were a prime target. For both the Plaza and Majestic the admissions had risen sharply in 1940 and kept rising. Cinema-going was the prime leisure time activity particularly for the women of Sevenoaks. For the men it was the town centre pubs – Chequers, Blackboy, Dorset, Royal Oak, Anchor, Blighs and Holmesdale Tavern

If the cinemas and pubs were important so were the two local newspapers, particularly the five-year old Sevenoaks News set up in Sevenoaks in 1935 by Donald and Edith Hooper during the Silver anniversary of the reign of George V. They had taken over the redundant three-storey Lime Tree Hotel and turned it into printing works with editorial offices. On the top floor were flats let out to local families.

Every week since the war began the Sevenoaks News had been vigilant in its desire to keep the town and villages in touch with the ongoing drama, although they were hampered considerably by wartime restrictions, a censorship which worked on a principle of self-enforcement. The newspapers were not allowed to give any information of military significance – including the whereabouts of bombing raids. This was designed to strike a balance between press freedom and national security.

On this dark October night the proprietors Donald and Edith Hooper were in their office in the Lime Tree Walk printing works. The war had taken away most of their editorial staff and the childless couple were working late into the evening as they prepared the next week's edition. Hooper, the editor, had enough copy to fill the paper over and over again but preference was being given to wartime news

The clock in the Lime Tree Walk printing works had already struck 10pm when the air raid alarm sounded. The Hoopers assessed the situation and decided to press on rather than spend the next few hours in the cold, damp cellar waiting for the 'all-clear'.

Enemy aircraft were heard overhead and then came the tell-tale sound of a whistle as a high explosive was dropped right over the town centre. As the noise of the whistle grew louder Mr Hooper fell to the ground and his wife, Edith took cover in the knee hole of her desk. The bomb tore through the building with a rending crash and exploded in the entrance porch. The Hoopers were plunged into darkness and found themselves bruised and ankle deep in plaster. The desk had collapsed across Edith's legs.

Above the printing works were the flats occupied by the Abbott and the Shorter families. As the building collapsed around them they hunted for clothes and waited for the rescue party to arrive. In all 14 people survived the Lime Tree bomb and, one by one, a few were lifted through the windows onto ladders by Sevenoaks Fire Brigade. The rest left calmly by what remained of the back staircase. Ambulances, police and wardens were all on hand.

Despite the censorship this was the biggest story in the newspaper's then four-year history. There was one problem. The linotype printing machines and the flat-bed press were damaged and the works and editorial offices were inhabitable. The Hoopers were shocked and confused but sufficiently aware that the details of the drama would appear in the opposition newspapers, the Chronicle and Messenger. From his home in Vine Court Road Mr Hooper explained the situation to his friend Eric Maskell, print manager of the Tonbridge Free Press, who immediately offered to print the Sevenoaks News. "It will be difficult", he said, "but

The front of the Lime Tree Hotel as it would have looked a few years before it was turned into printing works by Donald and Edith Hooper. The bomb which fell in October 1940 completely demolished the middle section of the building.

The printing works of the Sevenoaks News (formerly the Lime Tree Hotel) was eventually converted into attractive offices. Today it is known as the Sevenoaks Business Centre.

A picture taken soon after the bombing of Buckhurst Lane. The central section shows the site of the cottages after the rubble had been cleared away. The air raid shelters which ran parallel to the lane had also been demolished but the static water tank is clearly visible. So is the narrow entrance to the lane between two High Street shops, Timothy Whites and Achille Serre, the cleaners. There was also another narrow passage into Locks Yard (top left) and a gap opposite the Market House shows the shop which had to be demolished

His problem was how to look after his two young children deciding eventually to take heed of all air raid warnings and lead his family into the extensive cellars of Timothy Whites under the High Street. And that is where Roy, aged 10, and I spent many hours during the terrifying days and nights of 1940. We were in that cellar on the night of Thursday October 17th. In one large room lit by a single light bulb, amongst shelves packed with packets of nails and screws and more substantial hardware, were two single mattresses for me and my brother. My mother and father were in another room trying to listen to the wireless over the frequent wailing of the air raid sirens and the sound of approaching bombers. This substantial 200-year-old building, known locally as the Grey House and once a doctors' surgery shook as the bombs began to fall.

Less than one hundred yards away, in what was later described as "a small housing estate in a West Kent town," residents were peppered with high explosives. Families were sheltering when the bombs fell -- a woman and her grandson in a cupboard under the stairs which had been used as a larder. As they cowered in the darkness large pieces of shrapnel passed through a settee which was being used as a bed.

Two houses were destroyed but, miraculously, they were unoccupied as the families had gone to stay with relatives in Yorkshire. In another house the manager of a local cinema escaped uninjured when blast destroyed a house on the other side of the road.

Because of the censorship neither the Sevenoaks News nor Chronicle were able to give the name of this 'small housing estate' the following week. In fact there was no need because everyone who lived in the town knew this was Buckhurst Lane, on the site of what is today's bus station and car park.

The rescue services, already busy in Lime Tree Walk, were diverted to Buckhurst Lane supported by those from Tonbridge and Orpington. The scene which greeted them was of families emerging from their flats and cottages to be confronted with the sight of Buckhurst Lane on fire. People were wandering around dazed and confused, many in nightshirts. Policemen were attempting to bring order. Off duty wardens had come to help and at least 150 people were evacuated to safety.

It was only after the war that the full details of the raid were made known. "A lone German raider had dropped six bombs of a heavy calibre, cut a house in half and killed an elderly gentleman, shattered working class dwellings, rendered many families temporarily homeless and badly damaged water and gas mains. Families in the immediate vicinity were speedily aroused and told to leave their homes...."

Although I was too young to remember the finer details I was among those to be taken clear of the ever-expanding flames. Before the all-clear had sounded my mother and father, Florence and John Ogley, and my brother Roy and I were advised to leave our cellar below Timothy Whites and Taylors (now Boots) and find shelter elsewhere. The tiny Buckhurst Lane entrance into the High Street was impassable so, accompanied by neighbours, we walked down Webbs Alley into Knole Park and back through the main gates to the Royal Oak Hotel. It was typical of my father to head for a pub even in these dire circumstances but on arrival we joined all hotel guests in the cellar.

The scene in the centre of Sevenoaks the next morning was beyond belief. A large house had been cut in half by a high explosive. The homes known as Skinners Cottages were destroyed, never to be rebuilt. Knole Cottages and Taylors Cottages were badly damaged. Shops in the High Street, between Buckhurst Lane and Locks Yard, were still smouldering; the firemen had been there all night.

Another casualty was the depository belonging to the furniture shop of Youngs in the High Street on a site which today is opposite the Old Market House. The jagged, charred remains were eventually taken away leaving a huge gap in the row of High Street shops. In the 1960s it was rebuilt and today is occupied by Boots Opticians.

If it was impossible to imagine the full scene of devastation on this historic night there was more to come. In the early hours of Friday October 18th, another German bomb ripped through the roof of the Club Hall in the Dartford Road and crashed down onto the auditorium setting fire to the wooden stage and all the equipment. The exhausted members of the fire

Sevenoaks Constitutional Club, headquarters of Sevenoaks Conservative Association. Behind this building was the Club Hall, a building which provided seating for 600 people and was totally destroyed in a German bombing raid in 1940.

brigade, assisted by auxiliary firemen and other volunteers, now had to direct their attention onto Sevenoaks Constitutional Club, headquarters of Sevenoaks Conservative Association which was in danger of being enveloped by the flames now lighting up this part of Sevenoaks. Behind this building was a theatre, known as the Club Hall, which provided seating for 600 people.

So great was the fire and the smoke they could not save it. Firemen worked all night and into the next day concentrating all their efforts on saving the main building. By the morning there was a huge crowd of Sennockians watching the dying embers of the town's largest meeting place -- one which had been used by amateur dramatic clubs, local societies and visiting repertory companies for more than 50 years.

It was there that Sevenoaks Players gave their three performances annually and musical concerts were regularly planned. In 1935 a Sunday club had been opened for young people in an attempt to find an alternative to street corners and shop entrances. Advertisements in old copies of the local newspapers show how much the Club Hall was in demand.

During the South African war there had been patriotic events to raise money for the war effort. Soldiers who had been wounded at Spion Kop attended welcome-home meetings and

This drawing of Sevenoaks Constitutional Club shows how the Club Hall was attached to the building. It was destroyed by a German bomb in October 1940. The devastated area remained a bomb site for many years and when the rubble was eventually cleared away it became known by the people of Sevenoaks simply as the Club Hall bus stop.

a great party was held there following the opening of Sevenoaks Free Library in The Drive opposite in 1905.

When war broke out in 1939 the Club Hall did not close. In fact bookings for the various events were swelled by the soldiers billeted in Sevenoaks and, as the blitz increased in ferocity and bombs began to rain down on provincial towns, the shows went on.

No attempt was ever made to rebuild the Club Hall. It was too badly damaged so, in time, the charred timbers were removed revealing a bomb site and scar that was to exist for many more years. Eventually the area became an extension of the Vine Gardens with flower beds, a bridge and a fish pond. In 1988 a time capsule was buried deep in the earth with memorabilia of the Great Storm of 1987.

Some time ago I was given a copy of a letter written by Miss Evelyn Grant of 16 The Drive to her next door neighbour, Miss Hilda Downton, who had gone to Scotland to escape the worst of the blitz.

The letter was dated November 2nd, 1940 and in it Miss Grant described how a stick of bombs had landed rather too close for comfort. "One came down at the junction of Dartford Road and Seal Hollow Road, destroying the Club Hall", she wrote. "Another crashed in the front garden of my house.

"It must have come from the direction of the Hall as the earth and rockery are piled right up against my fence next to the boys' school. Parts of the bomb were found in their garden and some bits went right over the house. Marsh, my gardener, picked up a large piece on the road.

"The earth and some smaller rocks were also hurled onto and over the house but thanks to "shatter-proof" only three small windows were cracked....

"Thank God none of you were in your house to hear the terrific explosion and the rendering crash. It was at 1am Sunday October 20th, and I was asleep in bed. For a fraction of a second I thought my end had come but when the roof did not fall in I jumped up, slipped on my coat, seized my first aid bag and ran up to the town.

"I soon saw the Club Hall had received a direct hit by an HE (high explosive) and that the blast had blown in the windows of the cottages opposite. I called out to find whether anyone was hurt. I could see nothing but broken glass and debris of window frames etc. A warden also called and in the end people began to show themselves. They had been smothered in glass but not cut! I took three of them to my place.

"As I was waiting for them to gather up some clothes I heard a policeman say: 'Funny thing, a first aid worker dashed up to help and she does not know her own place has been bombed'. I asked him which number in The Drive and he said No 16! I told him it was safe to give shelter to these people".

In another letter Miss Grant told Miss Downton: "I went one night to the police but they were rude and asked a man (I think he was a warden) to see me home. He was dead drunk and at my gate took a bottle out of his pocket and asked me to take "a nip". I nearly hit him. I was furious.

"I often don't go to bed but sit in the lounge and listen, then go round the garden and up the road.....I put out a bomb at No 13, opposite. It was a terrible blaze near their garage.

"I still do four to eight hours daily at the post as well so I am beginning to feel the strain from lack of sleep — but we shall go on fighting just the same and "keep smiling.

"We never use the shelter as we feel the house is as safe, except for a direct hit and then the shelter would go too...."   Evelyn L. Grant

There were a lot of bleary-eyed people in Sevenoaks town on the morning of October 17th, 1940, especially those caught up in the raids, the spotters on the rooftops, who had spent the night gazing into the darkness for any signs of approaching aircraft, the wardens who had been knocking at doors warning of imminent attacks, the police and, of course, the fire brigade in Eardley Road.

In describing this terrible night the Sevenoaks News had this to say: "Although the town has suffered severely during the past few days (and the weekend was no exception) the spirit of the people has remained undaunted. In one bombed home people were putting things right, tidying up indoors despite the fact that the front of the house was completely open to the sky." Also open to the sky but never mentioned was the Sevenoaks News printing works in the former Lime Tree Hotel, the Club Hall by the Vine Gardens and many homes in Buckhurst Lane.

It is difficult to believe that the beleaguered people of Sevenoaks would have wanted to make the journey to the pictures on the night that Sevenoaks was so badly bombed. But many enthusiastic cinema-goers would not have known of the Luftwaffe's intentions and others were always happy to risk a few hours in the stalls. It so happened that on this terrible night the Majestic-Odeon was showing a real classic -- the *Grapes of Wrath*, a film directed by John Ford based on John Steinbeck's 1939 Pulitzer Prize-winning novel.

As they were watching Henry Fonda star in the brilliant story of an Oklahoma family of share-croppers, who had lost their farm during the Great Depression, a huge wave of enemy raiders were crossing the Channel. An air raid warning was immediately flashed on the screen and, as the film stopped, patrons bravely took cover under the roof of the circle.

Down the road at the Plaza was another classic – Errol Flynn, Bette Davis and Olivia de Havilland in *The Private Lives of Elizabeth and Essex* -- a film which had been nominated for five Academy awards in America. The story ended in tragedy but this was just a film. In the streets of Sevenoaks a real tragedy was unfolding.

It was only after the war that the details of this night became known. During the daylight hours of October 17th, the enemy had made four fighter raids over Kent some of which reached London and the Thames Estuary. Of the 300 fighter aircraft involved many carried bombs. After dark there were many more raids bringing the total to more than 130 killed and 128 seriously injured.

The Battle of Britain, as it was later described, came to an 'official' end on a damp and dismal day of almost constant drizzle on October 31st, 1940. Since the battle started in July Germany had lost more than 2,300 crewmen killed with 950 prisoners of war. RAF losses totalled just over 500, More than 1,800 German aircraft had been destroyed compared to just over 1,000 for the RAF.

November 1, 1940

The Luftwaffe, however, remained a force in being and hostile activity continued on November 1st, when 32 raids were plotted in London and the South-East.

London Road, Riverhead – a picture taken during the 1914-18 war. It was close to this spot that the village policeman, Pc Jim Farrell, was killed in November 1940. Other residents had lucky escapes when an oil bomb was dropped.

It resulted in six killed and 31 injured and among those who died were P.C. Jim Farrell and Edward Harrison of Riverhead.

Jim Farrell, aged 38, had been the village policeman for six years. He lived at 31, Chipstead Lane with his wife and two small daughters and was on duty in the village when a high explosive and two oil bombs fell between two bungalows on the London Road in Riverhead, Two other people were injured.

Among the Riverhead residents who escaped uninjured was the Sevenoaks RSPCA Inspector and his wife who were in the back of their house in the London Road when the bomb fell. The house collapsed around them but they were able to take cover and crawl under and over the debris. They were both taken to Sevenoaks Hospital and the wife was treated for shock. A confectionary shop in London Road, Riverhead was also hit but the shop owner and his wife had a narrow escape. In the house next door a woman and her son also escaped uninjured.

An oil bomb was also dropped that night and fell onto a car belonging to Mr A.E, Packman, the husband of the headmistress of St Hilary's School, Sevenoaks. The car was completely wrecked but no-one was injured. Another oil bomb fell in the car park of the Amherst Arms Hotel, Riverhead

The funeral of Pc Jim Farrell was held at St. Mary's Church, Riverhead a week or so after the bombing. More than 1,000 people attended including police, auxiliary fire service, wardens, the Home Guard and friends. Policemen from Sevenoaks formed a guard of honour as his coffin was carried into the church and the people of Riverhead collected a testimonial of £94 for his family with these words: "The village mourns the loss of one, who by his devotion to duty and kindly manner, endeared himself in the hearts of all with whom he came into contact."

Air-raid log

It is almost impossible to comprehend how many German bombers and fighters passed over Sevenoaks and district on their way to destroy the docks, factories and warehouses of London. On one night alone, in September 1940, a staggering force of 348 bombers and 617 fighters, along a 20-mile front, flew over our roof tops. The men on the observer posts found it difficult to believe their eyes.

In the face of the air-raid warnings, which sounded day after day, night after night, ordinary men and women showed amazing and sustained courage just by carrying on with their daily lives.

Don Brealey and his sister Pamela lived with their parents in Sundridge in 1940 and kept a pencilled log of the air-raid alerts on a sheet torn out of an old ledger. For those who were alive at the time that log brings back memories of four dramatic, tense months. For those who were not alive the statistics are barely believable.

Between August 13th, 1940, when Pamela began her daily vigil, until November 1st, when the Brealey family moved to another part of the country, there were 268 air raid warnings in Sundridge -- and that would have been the same for surrounding villages in the Sevenoaks rural administrative area. Generally, the siren would sound three times a day but often it was four times and, on occasions, six. There was a distinct pattern, roughly breakfast time, dinner time (we now call it lunch) and tea time.

The total of warnings over that period was 89 in the morning, 109 in the afternoon and 70 after 6pm.

Pamela also kept a note of the 'all-clear' which gave brief respite before the next wave of raiders appeared. The people of Sundridge threw themselves into a routine which was repeated everywhere. Some crouched in their Anderson shelters in the garden or crept under the Morrison indoors. Others used surface shelters in the street but the majority just carried on with their daily lives. They went to their offices or shops and, in the evening, many went to the cinema.

The log tells much about the increasing intensity of the raids. It was quiet at first and then, between August 19th and 23rd no air raid warnings at all. September 7th was the day that a German Dornier and a Spitfire Mk1 collided over the Sevenoaks side of the North Downs and the young Australian pilot Pat Hughes crashed at Dark's Farm, Dry Hill Lane.

On September 18th there were six air raid alerts, a total repeated on October 11th and 17th. Day time raids were bad, but at night it was unbearable. With the exception of just two nights there was not a single occasion between September 4th and November 1st when the wailing siren failed to arouse people from their sofas or beds. During this time many incendiaries, high explosives and parachute mines fell on Sevenoaks and district.

There were many more incidents and they continued well after 1940; in fact the villages of Sevenoaks and Dartford ended the war with the unenviable reputation as the most heavily bombed in Kent.

How our newspapers covered the war years

It is fascinating to see how the Sevenoaks Chronicle and Sevenoaks News covered the bombing of Sevenoaks in 1940. There was an embargo on any information being released that would give a clue to the exact whereabouts of explosions or crashed aircraft, unless they were German planes. However, readers at the time did not need to be told of the location because the gossip surrounding every major incident encouraged hordes of people to visit the scene.

The Sevenoaks News provided the best coverage because it was only interested in the local events, the Chronicle having to include stories from Tonbridge, Tunbridge Wells and even Crowborough. This meant that a few major incidents were hardly mentioned including the destruction of the Lime Tree Hotel. The bombing of the Club Hall, then our most popular event venue, was dismissed in a few paragraphs by the Chronicle.

There were plenty of the usual parochial stories including the surprise resignation of ARP (air raid precaution) controller, Mr A.G. Anderson, who became so heated over one debate that he simply walked out saying "I am fed up after what I have done for this town. I am resigning."

The chairman of Sevenoaks Urban Council in 1940 was Mr F.G. Humphrey who, in his inaugural address made it clear that his immediate object was to stop the German flag flying over Sevenoaks. He also approved the removal of a 1914-18 German field gun from the lawn outside the council offices in Argyle Road to the dismay of Sir John Laurie, who said it belonged to the Territorials.

It was not only the gun that was removed. So were 50 or 60 German and Austrian 'aliens' living in Sevenoaks – all rounded up in a dawn swoop on their homes by police. More tragic was the loss of a submarine minelayer which had been adopted by the parishioners of Seal. It was captured along with the crew of 55 in the waters between Denmark and Sweden.

The greatest controversy was the lack of surface shelters. There were a few in the town but people living in villages had to rely on cellars, if they had them, or just luck. The exception was at Chipstead where the local caves were converted into air raid shelters.

A big problem for the ARP wardens was souvenir hunters who were rapidly at the scene of every crashed aircraft, German of British. In October, one such man appeared in Sevenoaks magistrates' court accused of taking a rifle and a wrist watch from the body of a dead German, near Seal Hollow Road. He also took maps, log books and an oxygen outfit. Major Charles Pym, chairman of the bench, ordered them to be handed over.

The chairman was not too pleased with Agnes Walker of Bessels Green who appeared before the court for allowing a light to be seen in her kitchen at night. As her case was being heard she sat in the witness box knitting "for the troops."

Readers of both newspapers had plenty to say in the letters columns, particularly about the inadequate preparations for the anticipated invasion. Taking down signposts, surrounding Sevenoaks with weapon pits and road blocks and putting up steel shutters in public buildings was not sufficient for one reader. "Sevenoaks must wake up", he wrote. "The grey tower of St Nicholas Church, the white tower of St George's, Weald and the chalk pit at Polhill are landmarks that can be identified from the air. They must be camouflaged – NOW."

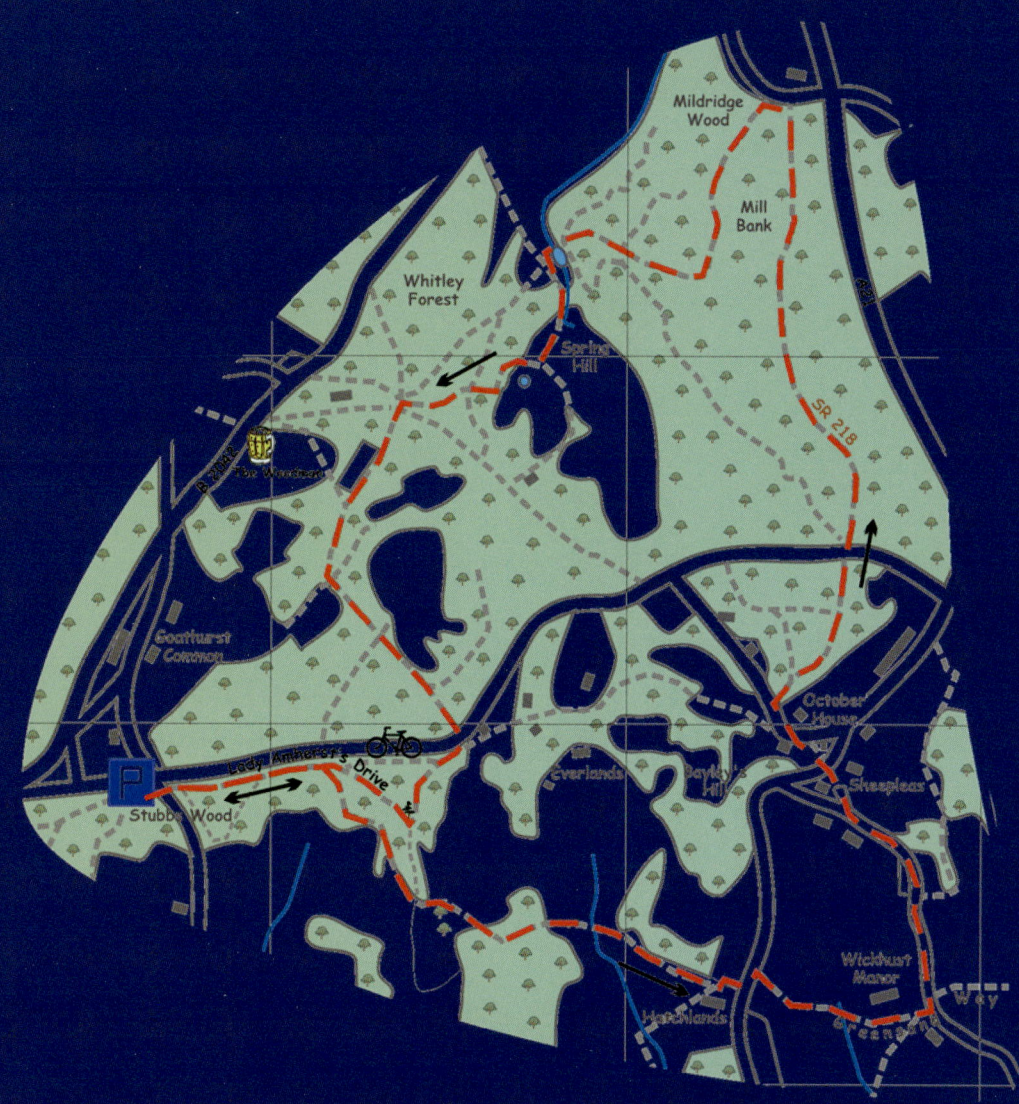

Whitley Forest, Ide Hill. During the war people were kept away by double rolls of barbed wire.

Whitley Forest in wartime

The area of Sevenoaks we know as Whitley Forest and Mill Bank Wood was out of bounds for most people during the war because this was a site where the army had built new roads and camps, created ammunition dumps and surrounded the area with barbed wire. There were Nissen huts and great security.

It is unclear when the army camp in Whitley Forest was constructed but it was certainly in use by the end of 1940 under the name of Forward Ammunition Depot. It was also a training camp used by the Royal Engineers and later the US Army 72nd Medium Regiment and the 24th and 28th Ordnance Bomb Disposal Squadrons. That alone gives some idea of the activity in the area.

As the war progressed the army began to stockpile ammunition in woodland areas rather than underground networks and the Whitley Forest provided sufficient camouflage for temporary storage. There were unlikely to be any attacks on a forest and the open air storage bays hidden among the trees would hardly be spotted from the air.

As the war progressed military movements increased and so did the size of the area that was out of bounds to the public. The site at Whitley eventually stretched to more than 2.5 miles with some 88 visible clusters of storage bays, seven emergency brick-built water tanks, some of which still remain. Local people, who used to walk the network of footpaths before the war, were kept out by double rolls of barbed wire.

Fern Warner (later to become my wife) lived in a house on Bayley's Hill that backed onto the heavily guarded Whitley Forest. Her father Richard, an actor destined to appear in more than 100 films and stage plays, was serving abroad as an army officer in 1940. Fern's mother was also an actress but on course to become a brilliant ceramic artist.

Fern, born in February 1940, was evacuated to Wales during the final year of the war but can recall the days when the soldiers had finally left in 1945. It was on the Whitley Forest army roads where she and her friends rode their bikes and enjoy the challenge of trying to crawl through the abandoned area of barbed wire without snagging clothes or limbs.

Mrs Olive Pilford, formerly of Croft Way, Sevenoaks and a student at Goldsmith's College is another who had clear memories of the countryside between her home and Ide Hill.

She remembered that, when the military vehicles left the site, there were about 10 deserted Nissen huts among the sweet chestnut trees and the local talk was of an ammunition dump but rolls and rolls of barbed wire kept her out.

As a child Mrs Pilford knew the people who lived at Whitley Mill. One of the girls helped her mother in the house while her brother cut the grass. They used to collect bunches of watercress from the millstream which was so welcome in wartime. And they took an old fashioned gardeners' water trolley down to the spring at Hammel pond to fill up with pure drinking water for their family.

On one occasion Mrs Pilford and her family were walking towards Ide Hill along footpaths and had to shelter in a ditch when aerial machine-gun fire was heard. They also heard a plane crashing some way off. On another walk a barrage balloon broke free of its moorings dragging its cable rather close to where they were hiding.

She remembered the Canadian bomb-disposal men, who were stationed nearby and how one officer entrusted her with his violin for safe-keeping when he went away on duty. After the war much of the area was taken over by English Woodland for tree felling and coppicing.

I still have a letter from a former Sevenoaks School boy who remembered the existence of a wartime ammunition dump at Whitley Forest. He chanced upon a "treasure trove" in one of the army Nissen huts in April 1943 and carefully, but rather recklessly, appropriated the lot.

The result of this exciting episode in a schoolboy's life was delight and admiration from classmates, a grilling from Ernie Groves, the housemaster at Johnsons, a visit by a Scotland Yard detective, confiscation of the entire cache and expulsion from the school.

In a detailed account of his adventures in Whitley Forest, P.J. Johnston wrote "A friend told me and Pat Harrington about the dump and gave us a rough map of its whereabouts, so one afternoon — wearing our biffs and blazers — we walked to the site, opened a five-bar gate, ignored the skull and crossbone sign and found a long row of open-ended Nissen huts with crates and boxes and metal containers.

A wonderful painting of Whitley Mill and farm by John Martin. The mill and the cottages fell into disrepair and were eventually demolished. This area was out of bounds during the army occupation of the area.

"Having filled our pockets with all manner of stuff and buried the rest, including detonators, rockets and flares, we put the explosives in our lockers in the JCR (junior common room) and in the ensuing days had great fun trying to fell trees at the rear of Johnsons by sticking gelignite around the trunks and lighting them. The matches failed to work.

"I hatched a plan to get our booty back to my mother's home, 143 Bradbourne Vale Road, and gave my "treasure map" to day boys, Jimmy Southworth, John Guntripp and Dennis Chambers, who were members of our gang.

"Sadly our presence at the dump had been reported by the residents of a nearby cottage and Ernie Groves asked to see us. A detective from Scotland Yard was also there and he wanted to know all about Whitley Wood. Having made various innocuous references such as - 'where would that be?' the truth poured out".

The game was up and so was Sevenoaks School for Messrs Johnston and Harrington. An army explosive specialist visited his home and found, not only the explosives, but also various unexploded cannon shells, incendiary bombs, piles of shrapnel, spent cartridges, bits of German aircraft, flares, window (the shredded foil used to disrupt radar), tear gas capsules and a mock-up of a Wellington bomber.

Mr Johnston told me: "We were both expelled and the day boys got six of the best. I was also put on probation for six months. I remember going to court and being represented by Mr House whose fee was £5".

Ide Hill Home Guard patrolled the ammunition dump during the war, fully prepared to deal with any would-be saboteurs. If they had been a little more vigilant they might have caught the boys and allowed them to enjoy a few more years at Sevenoaks School.

Lionel Barrow, who farmed the area around Ide Hill for many years, told me the dump was made up of an inner area surrounded by barbed wire with the main entrance opposite Gracious Lane and an outer area which took in Brooke Mound, the edge of Stubbs Wood, Sheephills, Seven Wents, the Riverhead Road round Whitley and Apps Bottom.

The Nissen huts were curved corrugated metal sheets dug into the bank where the ground was rising. There were many static water tanks (two survive at Seven Wents and the top of Douglas Hill) and the army lorries used the Everlands Drive as a level short cut rather than the hilly route on the Ide Hill road.

Ide Hill Home Guard, mostly 1914-18 war veterans, and those in reserved occupations, were quartered at Cox's Fields on the Edenbridge Road. There was a radio "beam" bending site at Ide Hill during the war".

The pub on the edge of the Whitley Forest which was popular among the soldiers, British and American, who worked in the area during the war years.

Quivering with immediate destruction! -- deer on the 11th fairway in Knole Park.

Knole on the bombers' route

Knole, unlike Whitley Forest, was not completely out of bounds during the early years of the war but for those who worked in the park or house it was an eerie experience to see the northern sky lit by the beams of the London Anti-Aircraft Territorial units at practice. For the Sackville family and their staff there was a gradual realisation that the town and the park lay on the bombers route to London.

If the world of Knole Park was changing so was this era of country house living. In June 1940 the writer James Pope-Hennessy was a visitor to Knole and described a stroll in the park and gardens. *"We walked in the evening light with wide turf alleys and rhododendron flowers and urns on pedestals….. but there was only an illusion of peace and the previous tranquil world and the whole ordered landscape seemed quivering with immediate destruction…"*

Knole Park did not close but many areas were out of bounds as a convoy of lorries filled with valuables from the house came out of the park, through the town and eventually on to the safety of a slate quarry in Wales. Silver in huge containers made another journey to a storage bank in Somerset.

During the Battle of Britain the staff at Knole took it in turns to be fire watchers. They were looking out for incendiary bombs and on the entrance tower there was a notice which read: "In the event of the tower being hit by a bomb descend by the rope."

Margaret Beavin was the daughter of one of the firewatchers. She remembered the searchlights sweeping the night sky, how the ack-ack guns cracked and how the park would be covered in metal strips dropped by the German bombers to confuse the radar system. One day she came across a German parachutist dangling from the branches of a tree. She also remembered the masses of lorries rumbling in the park from the army vehicle depot.

With the V1 flying bomb (doodlebug) and the V2 rocket which followed Hitler, brought the war to Britain as the Luftwaffe had done in 1940 and the German minister of Propaganda, Josef Goebbels boasted of the great destruction of London.

But Londoners and others throughout the south-east faced the onslaught with courage and a defiance that was, by 1944, their hallmark.

The story of the Doodlebugs and Rockets has been told in a book of that name with a wealth of photographs, maps and diagrams alongside stories of tragedy, endurance and courage.

It recreates the atmosphere of life as it was in those remarkable days between June 1944 and March 1945.

Doodlebugs and rockets

The years between 1941 and 1943 passed quietly and slowly with Sevenoaks gaining enormous recognition for supporting national appeals -- £480,000 for the warship HMS Gallant, £500,000 for Wings for Victory, £553,000 for Salute the Soldiers. The newspapers frequently carried stories of local boys who were missing, captured or killed and in 1943 Sir John Laurie of Rockdale became Lord Mayor of London.

On November 18th, 1943 the three-year reprieve from heavy bombing ended with a raid that left six people injured and an infant of 17 months dead on his mother's lap.

Then, as VE Day neared came the flying bomb, the doodlebug. Propelled by a pulse-jet engine it clattered just above roof top height and claimed the lives of many Sevenoaks people.

Thomas White of Bushes Road died on his way to work with his wife, buried under mountains of debris. Six more fell within a mile of Sevenoaks town centre. Beechmont, a rambling house built by the Lambarde family was completely destroyed when a flying bomb landed on the house. It was being used as a billet for the ATS girls billeted in Knole Park and two were killed.

A flying bomb destroyed the iron church of Kippington, one landed in Hollybush Lane recreation ground and neighbours were hurt by flying glass. The worst incident of all was at Crockham Hill where 22 children and eight nurses died when Weald House, requisitioned as a nursery, received a direct hit.

Appalling too were the deadly V2 rockets, launched in Holland and travelling at 3,500 miles an hour via the stratosphere. It was one of these which ended its deadly four-minute flight in Wickenden Road, Sevenoaks. It impacted on Nos 42 and 44, a pair of semi-detached houses, and blew them to pieces.

Nine people died in the debris of those shattered homes including an entire family, Leonard and Gladys Webb and their two children. Earl Beresford Moyce and his wife were also killed and so was Hilda Tomlin and her six-year-old daughter Rosemary. At No 49 on the other side of the road Hilda Kidd also died. In all 13 people were detained in hospital.

Two months later the war was over. It ended as it had begun – a town of damaged houses, covered in tarpaulin and rescue teams exhausted by their extraordinary efforts.

I have told the story of the doodlebugs and rockets in a book with that title. It covers the entire county of Kent with the famous map showing where they all landed, hence the brevity of this part of the war years.

The changing face of Sevenoaks

The Anchor, Dorset Street, Sevenoaks – thanks to landlord Barry, one of our great survivors

I am writing this story in the year of 2024. Christmas is approaching, the car parks are full and Sevenoaks is buzzing with people. They are not shopping in the way they would have been in wartime Sevenoaks, or the years that followed, because most of the independent grocery shops, the bakers and the butchers have, involuntarily, gone. Town centre Tesco has also been demolished to make way for a modern development of flats, so Waitrose has the supermarket monopoly in the High Street.

Many of the pubs have also gone leaving the ancient Chequers, the much-loved Anchor, and Blackboy and Blighs as the premier town-centre hostelries. In their place are restaurants, coffee shops, hair salons, nail bars, independent shops and one very popular department store, Marks and Spencers.

Sevenoaks is also experiencing the growth of e-commerce, so every so-often a vacant store has been taken over by a charity shop. It is a significant technological change that has impacted greatly on the daily lives of everyone who lives in, or near, this special town.

Few people today will know the full details of that terrible month in November 1940 when we lost half of the old Lime Tree Hotel, our major theatrical venue (the Club Hall) and the cottages in Buckhurst Avenue – none of them ever to be rebuilt. If it were not for the foresight of our benefactors perhaps they would never have existed.

It was Thomas Jackson and his father who bought land in the middle of Sevenoaks and earmarked it as a small working class community of 24 homes with 24 cottages, a coffee shop and a temperance hotel – Lime Tree Walk.

It was the Sackville family who gave sufficient land near the High Street in the late 19th century on which to build more homes for the working class, named after the birthplace of Thomas Sackville, the first of that family to live at Knole -- Buckhurst.

And it was also the Sackvilles who gave us the Vine cricket ground, the Vine gardens and an area of land sufficient to build a theatre – the Club Hall.

There are no plaques or memorial stones on these old bomb sites to describe their place in the history of Sevenoaks. So here is a small reminder of the role they played in our history.

A picture of Buckhurst Lane after the re-widening in the late 1950s. Cars are parked on the site of the old cottages – then destined to become the town's bus station and car park

Buckhurst Lane

When the war ended in 1945 no attempt was made to clear away the ruins of Buckhurst Lane. The cottages were standing but very little of them was left -- just blackened beams, tile-less roofs and jagged chimneys. Some items of furniture were still in the garden among the scattered bricks. Rose Cottage was a giant shell. The savagery was almost complete.

Central to this rubbish site was a static water tank, half full of stinking water and swimming with rubbish. Floating around the tank was a one-eyed teddy bear – once a child's loved possession and later a symbol of the Buckhurst bombing.

And so it remained until March 1955 when the Sevenoaks News showed its campaigning spirit by demanding that action be taken by Sevenoaks Urban Council to improve the site – even if it required an act of parliament to do so.

"Only 20 yards from the centre of Sevenoaks", it wrote, "are 1½ acres of stinking and rotting rubbish that would put an East End slum in the shade. It has been piling up for 12 years. What has been done about it? -- **nothing**. What is being done about it? -- **nobody knows.**

"The land appears to be the dumping ground for filth and garbage of the town. Rotting fruit and vegetables lie around in various stages of decay. It is a dump for dirty rags, a graveyard for worn-out pots and pans, factory waste and ashes.

"Its centre piece is a reeking war-time static water tank with five feet of stagnant filth. Children play on this urban rubbish heap. Everywhere are broken bottles and rusting tins. At one point is a sheer drop of four feet. Below is a collection of knife-edged bricks and glass".

The story included a picture of the area and comments from the residents of Buckhurst Avenue who said they could not open their windows in the summer because of the smell.

The reaction to the "scandal" was immediate. There were letters to the editor supporting the newspaper campaign and, at a special meeting of the Sevenoaks UDC the clerk, Mr A.C. Thwaites said the council was unable to prevent the public from desecrating the land. It belonged to the KCC and therefore was private property.

Within a few days Mrs Maude Davis, county councillor representing Sevenoaks town, was telling a full meeting of the KCC about the unofficial rubbish tip which was contaminating Sevenoaks, threatening the health of inhabitants and putting children at risk.

A dozen workmen descended on Buckhurst Lane almost immediately, taking away lorry load after lorry load of rotting rubbish. The task of clearing the site took several weeks. The inhabitants were overjoyed by the way in which the KCC had been stirred into action and appalled by the inactivity of the urban council.

The Buckhurst site slowly improved, the bombed area being turned into a car park. Two shops in the High Street, Chain Library and Achille Serre, cleaners, were demolished so that the entrance into the Lane could be widened. A new road from the High Street was opened which necessitated the demolition of both the Granada (formerly Plaza) cinema and the eight Taylors cottages.

The Grey House, home of Timothy Whites and Taylors was demolished and a new 1960s brick-built building opened in its place – Boots the chemist. Further down the lane Sevenoaks and District Old People's Welfare Committee erected a wooden hut named after their greatest benefactor Miss Dorothy Parrott, former UDC chairman.

In time Lady Boswell's playing fields became the site of a new library opened by MP Mark Wolfson in 1989 and the town's bus station moved into Buckhurst Lane. So did the town's famous Wednesday market.

Few people today who shop at Boots, or catch a bus, or borrow a book from the library, or park their car in Buckhurst Number One, will know of the bombing of October 1940. Or of the hell that was left in its wake.

Club Hall, Sevenoaks

When the Club Hall was destroyed on the night of October 7th, 1940, eight paragraphs appeared in the Sevenoaks Chronicle describing the drama of the night under a single-column headline. It was, after all, just another building hit by Nazi bombs and no-one was injured. It was empty at the time and likely to remain so for the duration of the war.

But this was actually the town's major centre of entertainment, accommodating 600 people and the venue for Sevenoaks Players' wonderfully supported thrice-annual performances.

Some years ago, Diana Wells-Brown of St Botolph's Road remembered how she danced on the stage of the Club Hall as a small child in the early 1930s. The weekly classes were run by a charming woman, Miss Everett, who presented a display of her pupils every year.

Her most lasting memory was the Dick Whittington pantomime in 1938 which became the talk of the town. It was financed by Hugh Meredith, who lived on Star Hill and his protégé, Keith Prouse. The plot revolved around many Sevenoaks places including Polhill, and the fairies in the show were terrified by King Rat, who later gave them all bracelets.

Diana was not given a bracelet and she was more than disappointed. She perked up a little a few years later when King Rat proposed and became her husband.

Apparently, Felix Tomlyn, a local dentist and artist, painted all the scenery and backcloths. When the hall was destroyed, leaving one wall standing, Felix painted a mural of a local scene which lasted until the hall made way for the extension to the Vine gardens.

The Sevenoaks Players and the Sevenoaks Orchestra (not Symphony in those days) performed all their shows at the Club Hall. The chairs were not raked other than a raised section near the back of the hall. The orchestra pit was at the front slightly below the stage.

John Dunlop in his book The Pleasant Town of Sevenoaks, writes about the young people of Sevenoaks who had nothing better to do in the 1930s than hang around street corners and shop entrances. "In 1935", he wrote, "the experiment was started at the Club Hall of a Sunday Club for young people but the shadow of war bought that to an end".

The rubble from the bombed site was taken away soon after the war ended and it remained an unspecified site until the Vine gardens were extended, with a bridge over a small pond and extensive planting. In 1988 a time capsule was buried deep in the earth containing memorabilia from the Great Storm of 1987, including drawings and stories written by local children, hand-made crafts from fallen trees and a few books.

There is no reference, in this part of the Vine Gardens, to the fact that this was the site of Sevenoaks' premier meeting place and theatre so, as a reminder, here are a few of the events which took place at the Club Hall.

December 12, 1915: Her Royal Highness the Princess Royal officiated over a sale of articles made by war disabled soldiers. The auction was conducted by the Countess Stanhope.

Thursday January 15, 1920: Sevenoaks Town Band held a concert and invited well known artistes to perform including Miss Camilla Cliff, New Zealand soprano. Tickets were 3s 6d and the Club Hall was packed to capacity.

Picture shows Sir Desmond Heap placing a scroll into a Time Capsule -- commemorating the Great Storm of October 1987 -- which was then buried deep into the earth in the Vine Gardens -- not to be opened for 100 years or more. Also in the capsule are books, essays written by children and objects they have made from fallen wood. The capsule exists on the very spot where the Club Hall once stood and is today an area of the gardens which has been transformed by Sevenoaks Town Council. It is now part of a community hub where key events will be held throughout the year including a Christmas Market. There is no mention in the gardens of the building destroyed in the bombing raids of 1940.

May 20, 1932: Dancing display in aid of the National Society for the protection of Children. Songs and arias provided by Mrs Lily Zaehner.

May 21, 1933: Boxing tournament, the main event being the bout between Gilbert Beadle and H.T. Hayman to be decided by a knockout. This fight, the programme declared, will last until there is just one man standing on his feet.

June 23, 1934: Sevenoaks Players' concert of Hiawatha was held under the patronage of Lord Saye and Sele. The conductor was Cicely Everts.

April 5, 1935: Film showing the activities of Fairbridge Farm School, Western Australia. From 1913 this was home to hundreds of children from English slums who travelled under various child migration schemes. The film showed how the school provided education in task-learning, husbandry, metal work and wood work.

July 1938: Major Branson, vice president of the Inner Magic Circle gave a display demonstrating his extraordinary sleight of hand.

The Lime Tree Temperance Hotel in 1885, headquarters of the local cycling clubs.

Lime Tree Temperance Hotel – Sevenoaks Business Centre

No-one was killed in the vicinity of the Club Hall on that night of November 1940 and no-on died in the Lime Tree Hotel which was virtually sliced in half – and that in itself was a miracle. Much of it was repaired but there was no money available to rebuild the central section. It continued as the printing works of the Sevenoaks News but the editorial offices remained at No 49 London Road until the newspaper was taken over in 1968.

However, it is still remembered by historians as the Lime Tree Temperance Hotel, built in the mid-19th century as a place for residents and guests to escape the greatest scourge of the time – cheap alcohol.

The proprietors advocated strict teetotalism and took in only guests who had signed the pledge, including nonconformists, members of the Band of Hope and Quakers. Their main responsibility was to persuade the menfolk never again to drink alcohol.

In 1885 the hotel embraced the Victorian craze for cycling and became the headquarters of the local touring club. A weather vane was placed on the roof of the building in the form of an early bicycle and remains there to this day.

The hotel was visited almost every weekend by scores of 'penny-farthings', tricycles and the new 'safety' pedal bikes. The Sevenoaks bike builder in those days was Mr Timberlake and his shop was at the entrance to Lime Tree Walk so business must have been good.

The large wheel 'penny farthing' was unstable on the rough roads of Sevenoaks district so Mr Timberlake introduced the safety cycle. On this machine both wheels were of the same, smaller diameter and the pedals drove the rear wheel via a chain and sprockets.

The hotel later became known as the Lime Tree Commercial Hotel and there was a tennis court and a croquet lawn in the grounds which attracted many visitors. It continued after the 1914-18 war but business gradually faded and it closed in the early 1930s, remaining empty until Donald Hooper acquired the building and set up his newspaper, the Sevenoaks News.

On the first floor he established the hot-metal linotype and monotype machines, the dominant global printing technology at the time, which allowed the Sevenoaks News to boast that it was the only newspaper printed in Sevenoaks. On the ground floor was an old flatbed printing press, set under a cylinder which held the newsprint and rolled over the type. This wonderful machine was bought second hand by Hooper when he introduced the newspaper in silver jubilee year 1935. It was made in Little Rock, Ohio but when and how it was shipped to England we may never know.

The editorial offices were also upstairs and the top floor was converted into flats. The Sevenoaks News operated from this building for four years – and the printers remained after the bombing of 1940. In 1966 the newspaper was taken over by Courier Newspapers (owners of the Sevenoaks Chronicle) and the old Lime Tree Hotel later became home of the Butter Council. In 1996 it was completely renovated and became home of Sevenoaks Business Centre.

The picture tells the story – the Odeon cinema (formerly Majestic-Odeon) salutes the victorious allied armed forces. It is a moment for the staff to celebrate with the rest of Sevenoaks – and here they are in victory mood.

Sevenoaks rural district ended the war with the unenviable reputation as the second (after Dartford) most heavily bombed area in Kent. More than 3,000 high explosives fell during 1,100 incidents. There were also 153 oil and 184 anti-personnel bombs.

Shoreham was known as bomb alley, almost 5400 high explosives and 22,000 bombs fell in that parish alone. During one February night in 1941 Shoreham received 45 high explosives and 16,000 incendiary bombs in the space of 20 minutes.

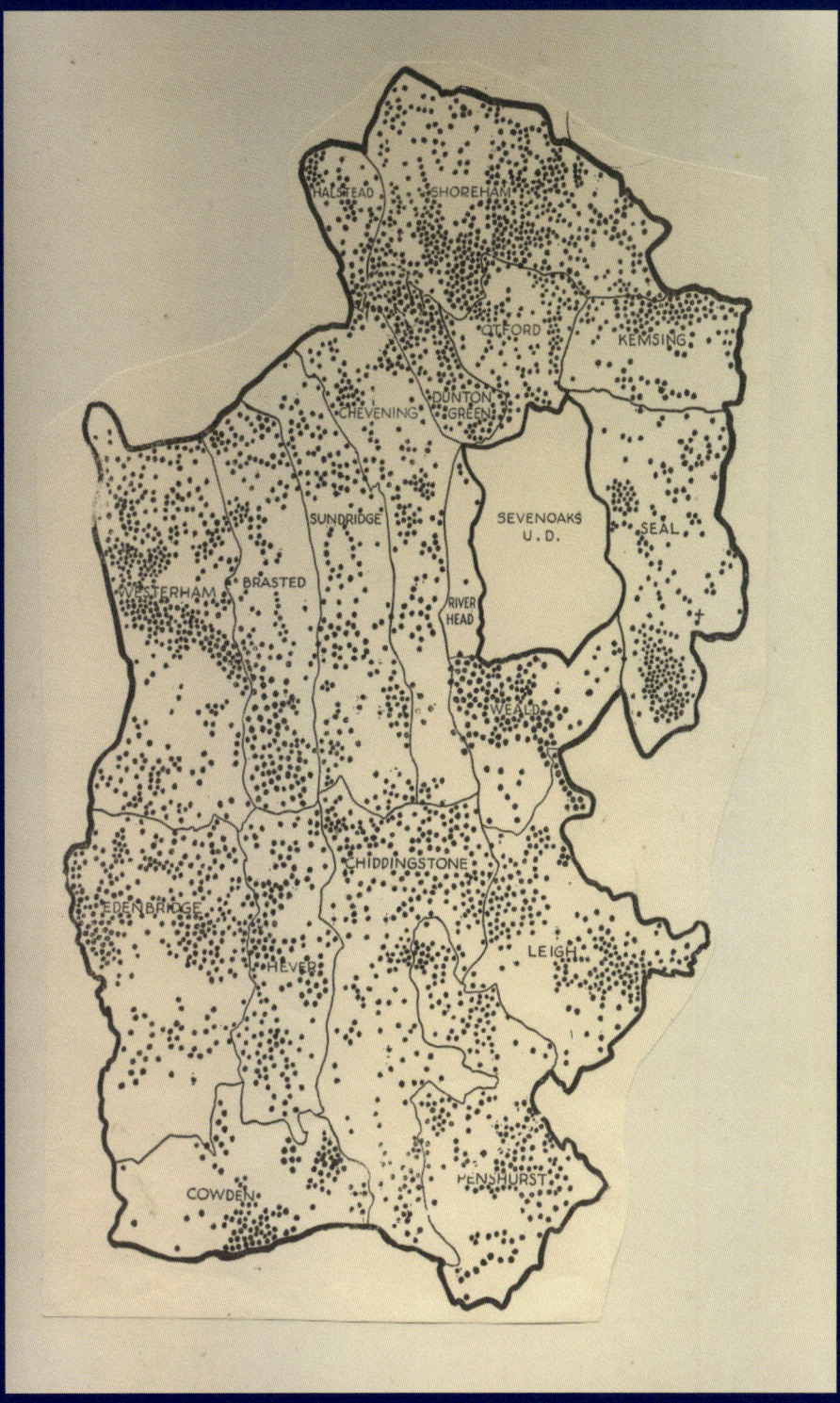

A BBC documentary after the war told how the village bore the brunt of Hitler's assault. Alongside the explosives 42 allied and enemy planes crashed in the rural area causing the deaths of 10 British and 17 German airmen.

Books by Bob Ogley

Kent – A Chronicle of the 20th Century

Volume One: 1900-1924

Paperback ISBN 1872337 19 8 ………..£12.99

Hardback ISNB 1 872337 24 4……… £16.99

Volume Two: 1923-1949

Paperback ISBN 1 872337 89 9………..£12.99

Hardback ISBN 1 872227 84 8……… £16.99

Volume Three: 1950-1974

Paperback ISBN 1 872337 11 2…… …£12.99

Hardback ISBN 972337 16 2…………£16.99

Volume Four 1975-1999

Paperback ISBN 872337 01 5……… ..£12.99

Hardback ISBN 872337 16 6…………£16.99

Biggin on the Bump

The most famous fighter station in the world

Paperback ISBN 1 872337 05 0 ……….£13.99

Doodlebugs and Rockets

Paperback 872337 21 8………………. £16.99

Kent at War

Paperback ISBN 1 872337 82 1…………...£13.99

Surrey at War

Paperback ISBN 972337 65 1……………..£13.99

In the Wake of the Hurricane

Paperback ISBN 0 872337 01 6 …………..£10.99

The Kent Weather Book

Paperback ISBN 1 872337……………......£12.99

Kent 1800-1899

Paperback ISBN 1872337 56 2……………£14.99

Bob and Fern Ogley

Bob was a journalist for 30 years until leaving the editorship of the Sevenoaks Chronicle in 1989 to become a publisher and author. The overnight success of his first book In the Wake of the Hurricane, which became a national bestseller, launched him into publishing in the most dramatic way.

Fern, a former actress (trained at Rada), a Volvo salesperson and a Yoga teacher, became a publisher and editor handling the 22 books written by Bob – and a few more by other writers.

Bob and Fern are proud that their books have raised more than £100,000 for such worthy causes as the National Trust, the RAF Benevolent Fund, the RNLI and Demelza House.